SHARING TREE SPACE

WITH HOT SPRINGS POET LAUREATE
KAI COGGIN

UNDERSTORY

The Sharing Tree Space Anthology

UNDERSTORY

The Sharing Tree Space Anthology

SHARING TREE SPACE involves partnering with Hot Springs National Park rangers, interpreters, and scientists to lead BIPOC and LGBTQ+ high school students on educational hikes focusing on specific natural world elements and writing poetry in the wild with them. The mission of this project is to engage them with the natural world, to facilitate community, and for marginalized youth to be seen, respected, held, and heard in their own personal authentic voices and valid experiences, thus combating societal and legislative erasures.

Each cohort of teens went on four wonder hikes on trails within Hot Springs National Park, with ROOTS and experts on each theme in accompaniment.

Hike One: Geology and Hot Springs Geothermal Waters
Hike Two: Green World (trees, flowers, mosses, lichen)
Hike Three: More Than Human World (animals, bugs, birds)
Hike Four: Unearthing Your Personal ARCHEOLOGY

SHARING TREE SPACE is a project created by the Inaugural Poet Laureate of Hot Springs Arkansas, Kai Coggin. Coggin was one of 22 poets across the nation to be awarded a $50,000 Academy of American Poet Laureate Fellowship in 2024. Sharing Tree Space was generously funded by the Mellon Foundation and the Academy of American Poets, with special deep thanks to community partner Dr. Margo McGehee Kelly.

academy of american poets

celebrating 90 years

 Mellon Foundation

Huge gratitude to the rangers, scientists, and interpreters of Hot Springs National Park: Ranger Madi Perry, Ranger Lissa Allen, Ranger Heather Adams, Hydrologist Jessica Vielman Cifuentes, Hydrologist Reilly Blackwell, Archeologist Victoria Reichard, and Virginia McDaniel from the United States Forest Service. Special thanks to Ranger Cane West and Hot Springs National Park Superintendent Laura Miller.

Thank you to the Arkansas State Library, the Arkansas Game and Fish Commission, the Arkansas Department of Transportation, the Arkansas Arts Council, Mid-America Arts Alliance, and the Arkansas Natural Heritage Commission for your resource contributions to the hiking bags for the young ones

Big love to my ROOTS, the young adult mentor poets from the Wednesday Night Poetry community, who accompanied me on these wonder hikes, and served as role models for the teen poets. Thank you Betty Brown, Geovanni Cisneros, Rowan Lay, Samm Binns, Melon Moon, Emeryn Phillips, Neelix Barby, Mandy Skaggs, Skyler Jay Shankles, and Christi Starr Sanchez.

Thank you to the Wednesday Night Poetry community for opening their hearts to the young teen poets to feature at the end of each cohort. And finally, thank you to Editor in Chief of Gnashing Teeth Publishing, Karen Cline-Tardiff, for giving these teens and their words a home.

In search of wonder,

Kai Coggin

Wednesday Night Poetry at Kollective Coffee + Tea is the longest running consecutive weekly open mic series in the country. Started by Bud Kenny February 1st, 1989, WNP has never missed a single Wednesday since — 1,925 nights and counting.. Kai Coggin has been the host since 2019. Every Wednesday. Open mic starts at 6:30pm. Join us.

Gnashing Teeth Publishing was founded in 2019 to showcase the work of emerging and underrepresented voices alongside writers who are well-established. As a respected independent press, Gnashing Teeth Publishing has a growing catalog of anthologies, chapbooks, and full-length books of poetry and fiction, in addition to several exclusive online features. Gnashing Teeth Publishing can be found online at http://gnashingteethpublishing.com and other online outlets. Visit http://linktr.ee/gnashingteethpublishing for more.

Table of Contents

for the trees

_____

Foreword

A version of this essay by Kai Coggin was published at the Academy of American Poets website, poets.org.

"You have no idea how healing of a space you created with Sharing Tree Space! It was truly amazing to see that queer people have a space to exist and grow old in this world. Being in nature and meeting Melon, Madi, Samm, Em, Geo, and witnessing the queer friendships and joy between them has been a life-changing experience! My life is more magical knowing people like you. Thank YOU so much!"

- Finneas, 18, 12th grade. Fall 2024 Cohort

Growing up, I was scared of nature, scared of the unknowns that lurked in the forest, scared of the creepy crawlies and wild things. Nature and I were distant acquaintances, certainly not friends, not the soulmates we are now. Born in Bangkok and raised in Houston, concrete jungles urban-sprawled the green spaces around me. The shrill sounds of traffic and capitalism's hustle and bustle sang loudly over birdsong. I was just trying to survive my youth and its Swiss Army Knife of traumas, knowing very young that I was not like the other girls. I had not yet owned the language of being queer, being gay, loving other girls, being Brown, being poor, being… just being. My teenage years were fight/flight/write. Poetry saved my life.

In high school, my crush kissed me on my 18th birthday, and her lips settled my cells into the language of my identity. In college, I was hazed by and kicked out of the Corps of Cadets at Texas A&M University for fraternizing with a female cadet and violating the *Don't Ask, Don't Tell* policy. I was punished, forced to march in my winter dress uniform in summer heat, around and around the quadrangle in from of 2,000 cadets. They made an example out of me. I had no safe spaces. I was isolated and scared, devastated and alone. I knew nothing of the trees. When I put the pieces of my young self back together and finally graduated with a degree in creative writing and poetry, a shift in my being moved naturally toward teaching and shaping the rest of my life into not just holding, but *being* a safe space, especially for LBGTQ+ youth.

In my early thirties, my distant green acquaintance and I came face to face. Nature suddenly became a friend, my new home. My wife and I moved, with our two little Fu dogs, from downtown Houston to a 17-acre wild slice of beauty in Hot Springs National Park, Arkansas. My relationship to nature became a part of my every day existence, and doors inside me that were once closed, suddenly opened and were flooded with trees, with songbirds and chipmunks, with dark skies of bright stars away from the city life. I became a country mouse— tender and healing the child inside me that never had a chance to stop and pick wildflowers or stare lovingly at a bullfrog. We spent years shaping the land, carving paths through the forest, building garden beds, planting an orchard of fruit trees. Nature moved so gently into my poems, planted itself, took root. My language as a poet was turning green.

Three years ago, following in my wife's footsteps, I became a Certified Master Naturalist, and during our field work, we would go on hikes through our national park to learn the names of the trees and flowers here, along with the hundreds of different wild species that populate this area. Another shift in my language unfolded—a tree was no longer just a tree, but a flowering dogwood, a serviceberry, white oak, eastern red cedar, ozark chinquapin. A flower was no longer just a flower. A bird was no longer a bird. The specificity of language in learning the names of all these species opened my heart up to another previously untouched level of my attentiveness, and again, there was healing. I began to see the world in a microcosm view, zooming in on the tiniest creatures while on my knees in reverence to that smallness, a wild species myself in the vast understory of our Ouachita National Forest. My language, again, greening deep and wide inside me, blooming.

To lean on the heartwood of my lesbian naturalist poet ancestor Mary Oliver, "I was a bride married to amazement. I was the bridegroom, taking the world into my arms." This world, *the natural world*, was never something that I had access to, was never a place where I felt I belonged. As a poor Brown Queer teenager in the city, I never felt like nature was open to me. When I did see nature, I saw only the white archetype of hikers and birders and conservationists. I never saw a reflection of me in nature, when I was young.

Now, as a woman starting to silver in my wisdom, nature is my sustaining lifeline. The mountains, and bubbling geothermal hot springs waters I drink, are my connection and grounding—my elemental force. The hundreds of thousands of trees are my guardians, my gentle giant friends. Their understory is *my* story. This land and all its more-than-human beings have held me and healed me. As U.S. Poet Laureate Ada Limón says, "We are not separate from nature. We *are* nature."

When I became the Inaugural Poet Laureate of Hot Springs in 2023, I wanted to reach the community in a deeper way than I already had been as the Host of Wednesday Night Poetry, the longest running weekly open mic series in the country. I wanted to merge my love for the natural world with my lifelong advocacy for marginalized youth. According to the

Trevor Project, if an LGBTQ+ teenager has one affirming adult in their life, it reduces the risk of suicide by 40%. One affirming adult. I wanted to be that adult to the LGBTQ+ teens in my community. I wanted to be the Gay Mama Bear Naturalist Poet to affirm them, to offer my hand and open up nature to them, too. This is where *Sharing Tree Space* was born.

Sharing Tree Space involves partnering with Hot Springs National Park Rangers, Interpreters, and scientists to lead BIPOC and LGBTQ+ high school students on educational wonder hikes focusing on specific natural world elements and writing poetry in the wild with them. The mission of this project is to engage them with the natural world, to facilitate community, and for marginalized youth to be seen, respected, held, and heard in their own personal authentic voices and valid experiences, thus combating societal and legislative erasures.

I knew this vision was a lofty idea, but when I was chosen as one of 22 Laureates to win an Academy of American Poets Laureate Fellowship, it meant this idea was a seed that others believed in, too, and I was determined to water that seed to bloom. I remember describing *Sharing Tree Space* to leadership of the National Endowment of the Arts, when we were all invited to speak in a round table discussion before reading at the National Book Festival in Washington DC. A member of the NEA staff came up to me in tears and said, "I wish my Trans daughter could go on wonder hikes with you." We hugged and I cried, too. I knew then the impact this project would make.

There were so many moving parts, but everyone I approached was absolutely on board, including Hot Springs National Park and three of its brilliant Rangers and the park

Archeologist. I gathered my ROOTS, young adult mentor poets in their twenties from Wednesday Night Poetry, who are also Queer, Trans, Black, and Brown. They would be there to show their enthusiasm for poetry, and so the teens could see a representation of themselves grown up. I reached out to a high school where I already had a relationship with the teachers, and after speaking to several classes, the Fall 2024 Cohort of fifteen teens filled up!

Our first hike was in early October, and when the teens approached the HSNP sign, I had a colorful assortment of hiking bags lined up for them, each filled with binoculars, a journal, pens, stickers, a magnifying glass and compass, as well as resources from agencies across the state. So many organizations wanted to show support for this project, and filled the hiking bags with swag. The Arkansas Department of Transportation sent in Wildflowers of Arkansas booklets and Ecoregion maps. The Arkansas Game and Fish Commission sent in Field Guides for Birds and Reptiles. The Arkansas Department of Natural Heritage sent in branded carabiners. The Arkansas State Library sent in Joy Harjo's latest collection, a hardback book of poems for each student. I couldn't wait to surprise the teens.

I'll never forget the moment I told them, "Go ahead and grab a hiking bag. Those are for you!" They shyly ran to the bags and their excitement filled the trees. "This is better than Christmas morning," a teen shouted as they dug into their bright purple bag. "All these agencies know that you are here, and they support you," I said, listing off the organizations with pride.

We all got in a circle and introduced ourselves with chosen names, pronouns, backgrounds all accepted in this shared tree space. It was a spectrum of beautiful and excited young people, and we ventured into the woods for our first hike centered on geology and the geothermal waters of Hot Springs. We found chipped novaculite stones from the native peoples of this land, and I taught them how to use their new binoculars on a high ridge of Hot Springs Mountain. All along the way, the Ranger shared scientific facts and history, and I pointed out beauty and modeled the practice of wonder and awe, stopping for them to notice a snail, a mushroom, listen for the woodpecker in the pine. We ventured back down the trail to the gurgling Hot Springs below, and sat together for poems. For each hike, I have a packet of curated poems around the elemental themes; poems written by contemporary poets who reflect the beautiful diversity of the cohort of teens. They could see themselves in these poets, and their poems about water, mountains, and stone. Together, we read. We shared space under trees and poems were born in the wild. It all came together, just as I had envisioned it, and the bubbling hot springs behind us sang a 4,400 year old song of healing.

There were three more hikes over the next three months—the green world (trees, flowers, plants, moss, fungi, lichen); the more-than-human world (mammals, birds, insects); and archeology (digging up our personal stories). With each hike, the teens got closer to each other, and their eyes opened to the natural world in the same way my eyes had opened. The tenderness and healing and acceptance took on a natural form in the shadows of trees. My walking stick became "the wonder stick," and we all passed it around. Whenever the holder saw something they wanted to share, or were curious about, or some wild blooming, we would all stop and gather around in awe, we would listen, then the stick was passed to another. It gave the teens, and even the ROOTS, agency in their own sense of wonder and the confidence to share it with others. We were bending over to touch moss, hugging trees, swooning together at the fiery beauty of autumn changing the landscape.

The Fall 2024 Cohort ended joyfully with a feature for the teens at Wednesday Night Poetry, where they read some of the poems that they had written over the course of our hikes, and the poems were collected for an anthology that will be published by Gnashing Teeth Publishing, an Arkansas publisher. The ROOTS, Rangers, and teens all became a tight knit family of poets, existing in the margins of society, but finding solace in the safe space of trees, knowing that natural world is theirs now, always. In all their spectrums of identity, they ARE nature.

"Being a part of Sharing Tree Space healed a part of me I thought would take longer to mend. I had felt disconnected from the Earth for months but just as the trees have an underground root system, I have found my connections, outstretched branches, my roots - me, a ROOT. A safe space where every person has a voice and is seen for their individuality and who they truly are. Sharing Tree Space brought us all together by nature, surrounded by the company of trees, leaves, moss, birds, goats, fungi, the wind, the stars, and the universe. Learning about the world around us helps us to better understand ourselves and those around us - a reminder that we are made of love, stardust and poetry."

- Melon, Young Adult Mentor Poet ROOT

"While I only spent a few hours with Kai, the ROOTS, and the students, it was abundantly clear to me the strength and the value this program was adding to all of their lives. It was an honor to be a part of

a program like Sharing Tree Space and I hope we are able to see more programs like this emerge in the future especially with potentially uncertain times for queer people in the United States on the horizon. As a student, I would have loved to have had a program like Sharing Tree Space and to have had mentors like the ROOTS and Kai in my life. I believe that the opportunity for personal growth, exploration and community building that Sharing Tree Space allows, is of great benefit to the students and their communities."

- Heather Adams, Ranger

Fast forward to now, middle March 2025. Since January 20th, the tides of progress are violently shifting backwards and the floor of democracy is crumbling at our feet. *Diversity*, *Equity*, and *Inclusion* are used as "woke" slurs, and according to the New York Times, agencies have flagged hundreds of words set to be purged from the government— words spanning from *accessible, breastfeed, Black, equality, female, gender, Gulf of Mexico, LGBTQ, Native American, pronouns, race, sense of belonging, they/them, transgender, underserved, victims,* and *women*. Erased from our governmental LANGUAGE. The *"T"* and *"Q"* were stripped from the Stonewall Historical Site and website, and now it reads *"LGB"* only. Erasure of our Trans and Queer history, which was bastioned by a Black Trans woman Marsha P. Johnson. Today, as I write this, crews are jackhammering the BLACK LIVES MATTER mural that once clearly defined a recognition and growth in Washington DC, after the summer of racial protest in 2020. From here, I can hear the sound of concrete and rubble, the breaking. Authoritarian rule and oligarchies are stripping away our federal workforce. The stability of our country is being dismantled before our eyes, and so much of what we love is being threatened and targeted for destruction. This morning, I talked another Transgender young adult friend off the proverbial ledge of suicide, the fifth friend since January.

Where in all this chaos is there room for poems? For touching moss, and young hearts blooming alongside tender spring wildflowers? For hikes with National Park Rangers, when thousands of them have been indiscriminately fired? Where is the space for a transgender teenager to hug an old growth pine tree and finally feel connected to the earth? An executive order calls for 280 million acres of our national forest and public lands to be clear-cut for timber. Sharing Tree Space. The trees. Our trees. Nature, my soulmate. *Drill, Drill, Drill!*

While recruiting for the Spring 2025 Cohort of Sharing Tree Space, I made a Facebook post after visiting our national park and meeting with a Ranger to plan and schedule the hike dates. I shared my smiling face in front of our national park buildings, along with the official Sharing Tree Space project description again to remind the surrounding community that registration was open.

After posting, leadership from the park reluctantly messaged me that it would be potentially compromising for them to be directly connected to programming supporting LGBTQ+ students, making it difficult for them in an already confusing administration transition period. Language. I understood. Because I value and love the Rangers and our national park, I immediately changed the outward facing language, in order to still be able to serve my precious young people. God, it broke my heart to edit the post to erase the words…

Sharing Tree Space involves partnering with Hot Springs National Park rangers, interpreters, and scientists to lead ~~BIPOC~~ and ~~LGBTQ+~~ high school students on educational wonder hikes focusing on specific natural world elements and writing poetry in the wild with them. The mission of this project is to engage them with the natural world, to facilitate community, and for ~~marginalized~~ youth to be seen, respected, held, and heard in their own personal authentic voices and valid experiences, ~~thus combating societal and legislative erasures~~.

The very demographic I am seeking to gather and take on wonder hikes was removed from the post. The language, whitewashed. But does that change my project? Hell no.

Though federal programs, funding, grants, and agencies are being stripped and canceled for their affiliation with diversity initiatives that serve the most vulnerable among us, as a private citizen, I am willing to origami my language so that this project and partnerships can continue. I know *Sharing Tree Space* saves young lives. There are hits we will take to our visionary hopes for the future, hits to the arts and artists, hits to our communities, hits to our livelihoods, but I have never been one to back down from my purpose. I am a community holder. I am a safe space. I have always spoken truth to power, but I will bend like a willow before I break. I have made my life out of language, and the language of trees will be holding my young ones again.

Over the last few weeks, I've spoken at high schools with my pride pin emblazoned on my blazer lapel like a Gay General, openly saying my wife painted the covers for my books, as I read them my poems on social justice issues they cared about. Hundreds of students opened up to poetry and to me. My new beautiful diverse cohort for Spring 2025 is built and over capacity, with teens coming from as far as Little Rock to join. My mentor poet ROOTS have grown from six to nine, ready to stand by the teens as examples of growing up and surviving. Rangers, Scientists, Naturalists, US Forest Service Biologists, and an Archeologist are waiting in the wings to walk in the woods with us. The trees will hold us. The spring breeze and smell of wildflowers will touch our faces. The healing waters of our hot springs will bubble up from the mountain into our hands. Young poets will blossom under trees as their hearts open to beauty, as nature becomes their friend, too. There will be curiosity. There will be community. There will be joy. There will be wonder. There will be awe.

Marginalized kids need to see marginalized adults that are happy, and silly, and curious, nerding out about a hawk feather or a mushroom. I'm not *indoctrinating* them, I am existing in nature alongside them saying, "Hey, look at this lichen growing on this rock—look at that resilience! We can grow, too, in this hard world. We can grow together."

poems

_____

April Adams (she/her)

Aprils Adams is a senior at the Arkansas School for Mathematics, Sciences, and the Arts (ASMSA). She was born in Ada, Oklahoma and calls Clinton, Arkansas home. She was homeschooled until 7th grade and is currently taking college classes through University of Arkansas Fort Smith. She started writing poetry when attending Wednesday Night Poetry, and it has since become her passion. She has won a Silver Key and an Honorary Mention in the Scholastic Art and Writing Awards.

Bough Abode

I take you for granted
It's been centuries since you were planted.

Residence of roots,
You've already rented me a room?
May I stand too, and stay with you?

The endeavor
Of your branches
Formed a mansion
In which I want to stay forever.

Hear

I stand here
Breezes twisting strands of hair
Bunnies trotting soil over there
Laughter found from these eyes
Leaves falling from the skies
Cars and chatter of animals echo into my ears
I stand, hear?

True Freedom

Two raccoons.

Fluffy and well-fed
The epitome of wealth
Oh, the irony.

I saw them asleep
Are they alone or content?
I only hope well.

Barred away from stars
How it hurts my fragile heart
They don't know the truth.

…

What *is* true freedom?

Two Haiku

1

Peaceful and happy
Amber leaves swaying in sound
Descending with grace.

2

I sense the greatness
Of Mother Nature's presence
It fills my soul whole.

Harmony Cole (she/her)

My name is Harmony Cole, and during Sharing Tree Space, I was a senior at Lake Hamilton High School. I have since graduated, and I'm now a college freshman. I've grown up surrounded by poets and artists in Hot Springs, Arkansas. I've never considered myself a poet, but instead as someone who loves history, community, and education.

Hiking Boots

I lace my hiking boots to prove something to myself—to feel
the pulse of a community.
Queer voices, bright and breathing, writers and artists moving
through the same light
I ache to be consumed by.

Differences so wide we build bridges,
not from obligation, but from something deeper—something
that lives in canvases, not paragraphs.

I want to be seen in a way I've never seen myself, yet my
boots are bound firm.

Each step carries its own confidence.
Each step trusts the ground—the way my pen trusts me when
it breaks open the earth.

Coaster

A slice of wood rests,
meant for words to bloom as poems—
I set down my drink.

Personal

I've never seen writing as personal,
never as private—my words have always felt communal.

Even here in the woods, miles from the seat where I tilt my
screen against prying eyes, and dim the light until it strains
my own-

I still feel watched
by the trees.

Grace Ann Conn (she/her)

Hi, my name is Grace Ann Conn and I'm a senior at the Arkansas School for Mathematics, Sciences, and the Arts (ASMSA), from Van Buren, Arkansas. My academic concentration is in environmental law, this semester some of my favorite classes are Ecology, French III, and Psychology. In my free time, I podcast, ground, and dabble in pickleball.

You to Me

I don't like my flaws
But yours make admiration
Grow above my heart

Hate my flaws, love yours
Spotted suns which run from the plain
Want your flaws as mine

Too many leaves to take
Falling on me I don't break
Fall please, I don't break

In my dream I leave
When I wake I want you here
Reach out to me, please

The leaves aren't the same
They miss your warmth, so do I
Reach for me, just try

Nothing New

I want you in the way
A toddler wants their safe, old, raggedy blanket
I don't love you
But I want to again

I want a person to think about
When I have to wait in line
To have dreams of
When everything real is burning down

But I think I'd cry at the sight of you
And run just far away
If there's ever a day
That we meet again

But I should choose my thoughts to be hollow
Instead of choosing to wallow
For you

But gosh

I love you
That's all I know

The Weather is with Me

I try to be small, yes
I am small
I am a woman

The sky grieves for me
It's tears pour over me
As I walk
Knowing I, myself
Am not able to cry

I have to be happy
Can't show sadness
People like happy

So the sky will do it for me
In hopes that I
Will feel ok
to cry too

Betty Brown, ROOT (she/her)

Betty Brown, a born and bred Hoosier called Hot Springs her second home for the past eight years. After finishing her undergraduate degree in Japanese Education at Ball State University, she taught English in Germany for a year through the Fulbright program. She then moved to Hot Springs in 2017 to teach Japanese at the Arkansas School of Mathematics, Science, and the Arts, which she greatly enjoyed. In August 2025, Betty left Hot Springs and ASMSA to embark on a new adventure in Florida with her husband, Dakota. While she is nervous about alligators and hurricanes, she is excited to see what this next chapter holds.

Teddy

Opening a new chapter often means revisiting the old
I overheard my mom telling the six year old
That has become infatuated with me this weekend
About my teddy bear
She tells her of how I slept with Teddy every night
Fell asleep to the notes from her music box
How I loved her so dearly
I realize that, as of yesterday, Teddy is in the basement
Had travelled back to Michigan
After traveling to Arkansas
And then traveling from my bed
To my dresser
To a tote
To a storage unit
I told myself it was for protection
From my cat's kneading claws
I believe myself
But am suspicious

The six year old accompanies me to the basement
Opens the tote with me
And I see Teddy for the first time in two years

I remember my mom comforting me
After I read the velveteen rabbit
Begging her to never ever burn Teddy
even if I was so sick that I died

The six year old carries her upstairs
I show her how to wind the music box
I kiss her on the head and she tucks her into bed

The Raspberries

No one planted the raspberries
They grew wild in the side yard
The International Friendship Gardens is nearby
Russia gave them some raspberry bushes
almost 100 years ago
I bet they came from there

When I was younger
My brother and I would pick raspberries
We'd grab old tupperware
Stained orange from microwaving spaghetti
And set off to the maze of bushes
And thorns to reap our harvest
He was always better at finding
The perfectly ripe ones
A deep red
Maroon, but not quite purple
You should eat the purple ones
As you pick them

Crouch down, look closely
Be careful not to get scratched
Look at the tiny hairs
Glistening in the golden sun
Gently piercing through the canopy
A spider scurries from behind
As the berry falls gently into your palm
Each pearl a slightly different color
Left behind on the stem, a milk-white cone
A bumpy bald bald head, with no more hat

Two in the tupperware,
And one for you
Until you can no longer see the spaghetti stains

For the pink, and orange, and red, and purple rubies
Take them inside
One bowl in the fridge
Use the other to make a cobbler with mom
I recently learned that it's actually a crisp, not a cobbler

One year, dad trimmed back the weeds
He forgot there were raspberries, too
In July, I still walk past the old step-van
Step on the never-used second-hand sailboat
Rocking, as I make my way over the waves of vines
Claiming the vessel into an earthy sea
To see if I can find even one
Tart, Russian berry
Let alone enough for a cobbler
That is actually a crisp.

in search of sunlight
a tree summits a boulder
to dance up a pine

Daymond Franklin (he/him)

Born and raised in rural Arkansas, I grew to love nature and its many intricacies. During this program, I was a senior at the Arkansas School for Mathematics, Sciences, and the Arts. Now I am a Biology student in college at the University of Arkansas, Fayetteville, where my work now is even more rooted in the nature of this earth.

Sharing Tree Space allowed for me to become even more appreciative and connected to the natural world. The community I built with the program is still a factor I dwell on often when I embark on my own journey in nature!

Memories Beneath Our Steps

Novaculite scattered across the trail,
etched with time's slow hand—
stones shaped for purpose,
now resting beneath quiet earth,
bearing witness to a history long passed.
Once tools, now whispers
of those who understood the land's deep rhythm.

The trail leads us forward,
through roots and fallen leaves,
where the earth holds more than just rock—
it holds memory,
tucked between each layer of soil,
suspended in the silence of nature's voice.

Then, from the depths, the springs rise—
warm, breathing softly into the air,
like a pulse carried through the earth.
Once thought to heal,
they still rise to offer comfort,
soft steam lifting toward the sky—
the earth's breath, steady, patient,
releasing warmth like a forgotten promise,
still reaching to touch those who stand still enough to feel.

*Poet's note: The poem reflects our first hike, where we delved
into the history of the park, learned about novaculite rocks,
and explored the ancient belief in the healing properties of
the thermal springs.*

Freedom of the Trapped We See

"Free," a term for those
who lack the weight of chains on who they are.
"Free," a word that releases what's confined
the moment it's spoken
into this beautiful world we see.

"Free," like the caged creatures here,
bringing joy to the faces of those who watch them.
"Free"? That can't be.

These creatures aren't free to graze,
to wander the endless grass at their hooves.
Not free to move sleekly through woods
on paws meant for the forest floor,
or to slice through the air,
wings wide, beaks peaked,
soaring the skies vast and wild.
No—these creatures are trapped.

Trapped—a word for those denied
the unweighted glory of being free.
Trapped—a word that binds,
keeping escape at bay.
Trapped, like a box that hides
that wild spirit inside.

Yes, these creatures are trapped,
bound by the mercy of their captors 'hands,
confined in small enclosures,
their reach stolen from the world ahead.

Dependent on the will of others,
yet still the wild thrills in their hearts.

This shouldn't be.
Return them to the earth they seek—
the swamps, the forests, the fields,
the places where they thrive,
where they were meant to survive.

Let them be free.
Free—are we free?
Free—are they free?
Free. Let them be free.

Poet's note: This poem was written during the third Sharing Tree Space hike, although it was my second experience with the program. The theme of the hike, if I recall correctly, centered on the living world. We visited the Alligator Petting Zoo, where we observed both the remarkable beauty of the animals and the controversial conditions in which they were kept. While I certainly appreciated seeing these creatures firsthand, I couldn't help but feel a deep sense of sympathy for them, acknowledging the challenging reality of their current circumstances. This poem reflects that initial admiration, followed by the somber realization that these animals are not in their rightful place.

Finneas Salazar (he/him)

My name is Finneas and I have a passion for ecology and conservation biology. I grew up around the south and ended up in Hot Springs, Arkansas while attending ASMSA for high school. I started writing poetry as an outlet to express my appreciation for the natural world and as a way to process my feelings about the current political climate of the US. I am currently studying wildlife and conservation biology at Southern Arkansas University, but I hope to continue to bring a love of art and poetry into all aspects of my life.

The Monster

I think there's a monster in my closet
I was told it is prude and ugly
Its name unknown
It is not to be mentioned

Don't even go near the room
It will try to convince you to unleash it
But at night when the TV is off and the house is quiet
I swear I hear crying coming from inside
It sounds like a boy my age
But what happens if he escapes

They told me never to look inside
But the cries get louder
And harder to ignore

I think there's a boy in my closet
I can't ignore
the door
My hand
Reaches
And unlocks
And opens

A child is in the corner
Malnourished and scared
He is just a boy
With the same eyes I see
In the mirror
And in dreams

Did they know the monster looked like me?
How can he be so young
so innocent
And called such words

I'm starting to think there was no monster in the closet
Just a boy wanting to be let out of the dark
And unleashed from the
Loneliness

Dendritic Friend

I made a friend the other day
She's tall and peaceful
With hair that blows in the wind

She is one with the forest
She is a friend of many

I only met her the other day
But she's strong and wise
And kind

When we first met
She didn't tell me her name
But I've known her for a long time

She was nice with the birds
Her soul is a home for many
She shows her years in her marks but her spirit is youthful

I haven't seen her since that day
I hope she is doing well
I know she's probably made many friends since
and had many well before I came along

I am not first to admire her beauty
I hope I will not be the last
For she is a good friend

Lemurs

Tail swinging
gracefully prowling
monch monch
No table manners
No tables :(

Pen

I dance on the page
A piece of me is left behind
I hope I was good

Making this with you
Guide me, lead me to create
Take 'till I'm gone

Tree haiku

A tree is just that
No need for anything more
Just tall, green, alive

41

Melon Moon, ROOT (they/them)

Melon Moon. 25 years old. Hot Springs, Arkansas. I am nonbinary, pansexual, & a fiery Aries. I've been a writer since I was 13 years old. It helps rattle the goo & ooze out of the brain and be painted colorfully onto a sheet of paper instead. I love writing, singing, painting, doodling, drinking hot tea with honey, reading manga and graphic novels, playing video games & spending time with friends.

colored pencil shavings float in red wine
hands smudged black
a rainbow carpets my living room,
as the canvas finally finds rest on the floor

the sun cradles three steel tongue drums,
two ukuleles and one toothbrush
i am reminded of unconditional love,
snapchat streaks appearing without intention,
that fresh, crisp consistency that comes with friendships you
hope will last
the clock reads 1:11am,
bon iver's holocene and nicotine
and
a curled oval of sleep
the sleep starts to creep
behind my eyes

the skeleton sits in an upright position,
hands in prayer against its ribcage
if a statue can find a state of mindfulness
despite its lack of life and breath
then may we all practice the same?
i spot my yellow vans
untied and worn,
grounded today by the earth

today
i saw
a gaggle of gals,
group of giddy pals, smiles budding
magnolia, chinese fir, oak, sycamore and redbud trees —
roots firmly planted in the soil

moss succulent and bright from the recent rains
resurrection fern and figs and fidus achates
a leaf hole-punched by a hungry bug

today
i heard
the call of a carolina wren
the bleating of goats as they welcomed us as their own,
mouths suckling softly on our pant legs,
misting our hair wet with dew
and warm laughter echoing
from the sheer joy of our shared gift of nature

i picked up the pen to write tonight but
my body now begs for a pillow
underneath my delicate head
i set a reminder to purchase wind-chimes

all of us, moons
wolves howl at our radiance

"young alligators are best suited for making
purses and shoes,"

a fact noted in a petting zoo
still as statues, basking in the hot sun
their breath and very existence
looked over by humans that are cruel

Mockingbird

Today I heard the song of a bird from outside of my kitchen window as I made scrambled eggs on the gaslit stove.

Still on the search to discover which one made the call, I thought it was a mockingbird — Arkansas' state bird, and as I found a video of one happily chirping in a tree, I felt tears swell in my eyes —something had awakened in me.

I heard a mockingbird and suddenly I was in my parent's mobile home, sitting silent in the country 25 minutes outside of town.

I heard a mockingbird and my mom's laugh in the striped fold out chair. Smelled coconut oil and pink mimosas carried by the wind to kiss the Earth.

I heard a mockingbird and the strum of a ukulele and my own voice — smaller and untuned, but still my own.

I heard a mockingbird and the gentle shut of a screen door as my dad entered the house for food after working since noon. I heard the hum of a fridge and the taste of sweet peach iced tea.

I heard a mockingbird and felt the humidity.

I heard a mockingbird and somehow I think it heard me.

I came to find that the tune was not one of a mockingbird
so I searched,
wondered,
listened
to bird calls on Youtube
and I found her
finally—
t'was the trill of a white-throated sparrow.

I hear her song every day now, from the tree leaning onto my
balcony, harmonizing with the rooster next door,

I adore her melody.

Blessed by the birds every morn.
Smiles painting my face,
gifting the feeling of being reborn.

Cameron Crowder (he/they)

Cameron Crowder, a soon-to-be honors graduate from Little Rock Central High School, draws from his experience as a homeschooler and trans man in his writing. He credits his love for reading and writing to his wonderful mom, who, all throughout his life, advocates for and nurtures his voice and self-expression. In his free time away from studying his favorite subjects, Spanish and Biology, Cameron loves trading poetry with his girlfriend, Vienna, as well as reading, painting, running, and exploring the outdoors.

Threatened by Wild Things

Two car rides later,
I slammed the book down.
The unruly kitchen gnat,
smaller than most,
I smashed
and rolled into a ball.

This time my conscience fought back,
tidal roar in my ear.
An angry whoosh of cerebrospinal fluid.

I kept my little ones safe and fed tonight.
Now, to tuck in my inner child.

Drinking Again

my new love's flasks are full of honey instead of gin
i don't need to numb myself from anything
she can make my head spin with just her eyes
she'll leave pretty purple poems on my neck

Safe Spaces

I dream of a reality
where no one exists beyond who they were
before the world's evil shaped them:
every centipede eating someone's hope in their pocket fades
away like mist when the sun
reaches the top of the sky.

At the horizon,
there's a tiny cabin with two people who,
despite their young exteriors, have enough wisdom and
potential to fill thousands of libraries.

They don't need anything
but each other's presence as entertainment,
they're fond of creating their own experiences
they sculpt the ground to accommodate their creativity
cutting and weaving it into a second oasis

Gems

After page after page of scrambling to succeed
with a broken pencil,
ink spills out of me.
I'll investigate the error.
To wander around the labyrinth
of my consciousness is to slip my hands
into my grandmother's worn denim couch cushions
unsure of
but always grateful for
the gems I'll find

Here Again

And then suddenly
my dad is having panic attacks this time
I'm calm like stagnant water.
When he gathers his strength, he stoops down
says I love you, voice cracking—
my voice cracks too, and I feel truly myself.
NFL arms wrap me tightly, hold me to his shoulder
he becomes tall again,
And I become even shorter than before when he holds my
head so he can kiss it
And then suddenly I am a little girl again
And this time it doesn't hurt

Vienna Lewis (she/her)

Vienna Lewis is a senior at Little Rock Central High School, and a proud trans woman. At Central, she is the choir president, as well as the music director for theatre. When writing, she picks each word carefully, striving to invoke strong images and emotions. When she's not obsessing over music, she's with her best friend, Betsy, and her boyfriend of 3 years, Cameron. After high school, she wants to get her bachelor's in Vocal Music Education, to support a career in music.

As you slip out from my side,
I hear the loneliness whir and beep twice into place.
Grabbing whatever's closest, I would carve the flesh
from my skin to hear blinds dance on glass.
The water in my ear convinces
that it's happening as we speak.
Instead the glass beads giving me shape spill
and pop against the floor.
Their purpose served,
to keep whatever shape I molded myself into; to stop
the wrinkles from setting in.
The Flames meet the Tides.
My movement intrinsic.
Your's ethereal.
I've been given my task, I know what I will do.
You are limitless, flowing without reason.
We are prodded at all the same.
To make me fester and you move.
All we can do is learn and sizzle away.

I want the woodland on me.
Dipped in pond water.
The fear caking on honeysuckle,
to sugarcoat my wounds,
like orange peels, cut and boiled.
Flowers take root.
Sunshine on my body.
God and Nature will wash my hair,
the frizz of my life calmed,
the curl of my soul nurtured.
His mother watched him cut my hair and bowed her head.
I gave all I can give.
The swirl of analytical words
and numbers flush down my back.
They laugh as my last mumbling means nothing.
They pick me up off the forest floor
and hold me in Their arms.

I smell riding on the lawn mower with my grandpa.
He can't see me now,
but if he could I hope he can see that I'm happy.
I think I'm happy.
Feel an itch and count the reasons
why he doesn't love me.
Surrounded by a new family.
I can't feel the sun on my skin, only the smoke of burning
leaves in my lungs.

Kayden Forrest (he/they/xe)

Kayden Forrest is a writer from Paragould, Arkansas. He recently graduated from the Arkansas School for Mathematics, Sciences, and the Arts, and is now studying Political Science at the University of Arkansas at Little Rock. He began writing poetry during his early teen years, now writing about identity and life as a disabled transgender person. He hopes to practice civil rights law in the future.

Nature's Reminders

The wind blows
on my bare arms
and through my hair.

And I realize
how lucky I am
to live among the beauty of nature.

How grateful I can be
to see the rippling water,
Even if I cannot feel it myself.

A goat came up to me,
Tapped my hand with its nose
Even though I cannot go in its enclosure.

And I wonder if that
was nature reminding me
that I am allowed to exist here.

I Want to be Near the Water

I want to be near the water
Feel it rush against my bare hand
Cold and fast, if only I could stand
Yet, instead, I'm on land

Still, the water calls for me.
Babbling brooks
Across the rocky nooks,
As I sit, my hands gripping this notebook

Creaks and rivers,
Oceans and lakes,
Childhood memories it would make
Oh, how my heart aches

For serenity
For calm
For a piece nature in my palm

Take a photo for me, please?

I Never Cared for Bugs

I never cared for bugs,
Always disgusted, creeped out, or scared

I never cared for bugs,
Squishing the ones I wasn't too afraid of

I never cared for bugs
Until I saw an entomologist's passion, with moths on the
walls

I never cared for bugs,
But then I caught myself avoiding squishing them with my
wheelchair

I never cared for bugs.
Not until I met you.

I Think the Rain Would Fix Me

I think the rain would fix me,
The earthy smell filling the air
Taking away everything else

I think the rain would fix me
First few drops splashing on my face
Turned upwards towards the sky

I think the rain would fix me
Soaking me with rainwater
Washing my pains away

I think the rain would fix me.
Because the rain is nature's reminder
That we are still alive.

To Those Blamed Before Me

Young one,

Do not let the words of others
dictate your view of yourself.

Do not let their harshness
keep you from being soft.

Your existence is beautiful,
despite those who deem it unworthy.

Your body is sacred,
despite those who say otherwise.

This burden, this blame,
It is not yours to carry.

Throw it in the flames.
Rise from the ashes.

Continue fighting
Even when others tell you to stop.

Young one,
Live again.

Geovanni Cisneros, ROOT (he/him)

Geovanni J. Cisneros or (Geo) uses he/ him pronouns and is a 28 year old Trans poet. He is a chef who finds and shares healing through creative expression, whether that be through words or cooking. A spiritual person drawn to nature and stones, he brings warmth and generosity to his work and relationships. His poetry explores themes of identity, community, and the natural world. When not writing or in the kitchen, you'll find him singing karaoke with friends or wandering outside among the trees.

Mothers

My Mother…

Toughened me
Threatened me
& Taught me,
all of what not to be

Mother Nature…

Nurtured
Cradled
& Loved me,
showed me all that I should be.

Just Be

I woke up, but I was not awake.
I put on clothes for the day, but I didn't not get dressed
I brushed my hair and teeth
Yet Nothing felt clean
I went out to the world and I did not feel seen.

But ....Oh the beauty of our mentor here in Hot Springs.
  A brown Lesbian that dare not let me go unseen.
A catalyst in the community. Unchanged by hate

You brought me and my family together.

You are my family …
… us all here together.

You united us with one another

You created a new town for me.

A new way for me
to in this world be.

Just be

Just
Be

Just be.

Grazing Deer

On a beautiful hike through the mountain
The deer were grazing.
They were Gracing me.
Gracing me with their beauty.
Grazing, just getting something to eat.

They stood there quiet
Eating, grazing,
Light crunching of leaves beneath them
Sharing their tree space with me.

Gracing me.

Toxic

You take my breath away,
but not in a way I want you to.
You hug me tight and don't let go,
but not in a way I need you to.
You keep me together and composed,
but not in a way I appreciate.

You want to stick around
longer than you should stay…
and that can get pretty toxic, I must say.

Yet—
" I hold the power"
to let you go, take you off, so to say.

Isn't this how toxic relationships go anyway?!

But—
I can't have you go away,
I need YOU so I can function on a day to day…
I can't go out in public,
without YOU as my safety net.

I can't bear the worry of the world coming for me
if I don't blend in.

Even if you are harmful,
uncomfortable,
uptight, and manipulative,
I cant leave you,

I don't feel safe without you,
I'm not myself without you.

Even if you make me want to drive off the road in a rage
because you are not keeping your promises to me,
as you say.
You keep lying and lying to me,
and I just swallow my sorrows and lament,
because the very next day, I'll commit to you again.

I have to cut out these parts of my being
that are not meant for me,
So I'll finally be able to let you go, and set me free.

But in the meantime,
in the meantime
I keep coming back
and back again
because
you take my breath away—

an ode to my chest binder.

Peace

What I feel on nights like these,
at the age of 28,
I am finally free,
doing things I should have done at 21, 22, 23,
living my living genuinely,
sharing spaces I never did

From days that hold hikes,
wonder, and expeditions
to
nights at places that have never felt inviting
to my dysphoria because the "scary men"
are standing at the entrance

I am finding that there's allies who,
by appearance, don't seem to be...

So much wonder in my days
that carry so much love with no prior
expectations or conditions

Love and acceptance
without a transactional requisition

Peace filled days with beautiful meditations
as daily invocations to the universe
stay in communication

Like the network of roots
we are intricately winding

and intertwining together to find connection
all of us thriving for growth and direction.

Living the life I never could imagine
or mention

Being in the right time at the right place

A Village

It apparently takes a village
for so many different things
to help find your self
the way you were meant to be.

It takes a village
reflecting back from you
to allow the magic that shines to be seen,
seen from within and sang to the wind.

It takes a village nowadays to show our children
that their words are valid,
that they hold power in who they are
that their identities matter
that their actions matter.

It just takes a village to show them
that the whole world is not against them
that not all is lost and hope is within us.

It takes a village
to raise a loving person in one's self
to raise the artist, the poet, and the lover
all the way from the pits of hell.

It takes a village,
taking care of each other,
To realize what we deserve from
one another,
The standards of love and respect
we are to be held to.

It takes a whole village....
One I never thought I deserved

But they know I'm deserving
and they deserve me too.

KC Cavin (she/he)

My name is Katelynn, but most people call me KC. I have always seen the beauty in the quiet parts of life. Poetry has become a passion of mine, sparked by those from the Wednesday Night Poetry community and Sharing Tree Space. Outside of poetry, I am an artist and musician, but I plan on becoming a math teacher. I am from Jacksonville, North Carolina and I'm a senior at the Arkansas School for Mathematics, Sciences, and the Arts.

Moving Out

I'm still somewhere in my mother's house
somewhere in the back of the family photos
pinned on the fridge with alphabet magnets

I'm still somewhere in my mother's house
where the new meets the old
where the rooms all get cold
because she keeps it at 65 degrees

I'm still somewhere in my mother's house
I'm the doll sitting on my sister's shelf
I'm the books on the coffee table
I'm the blankets thrown haphazardly across the couch
I'm the dust on top of the cabinets

I'm still somewhere in my mother's house
forever her little girl

Echoes

I write your name on my hand with marker
Scribbled in the margins of my sketchbook
Doodle our initials in a heart
I listen to our song over and over
Close my eyes and try not to look
Pause, rewind, restart

i trace your name into my skin
Your name forever engraved herein
I whisper it into the night
Echoes dancing away into the light

I can still smell you in my sheets
Your scent lingering in the air
A memory of what used to breathe
The taste of your lips, still so sweet
Please stop, this isn't fair
How can you forget me with such ease?

You've touched my soul so gently
Flooded all my senses, not hesitantly
One last moment is all I ask for
One last kiss is all I'm good for

Images

Your idea of perfect is the girl I used to be
the one that was whimsical and free
not a care in the world except that
calculus homework was due
My idea of perfect is you
just as you are
in this moment, the past, the future
the good, the bad, the ugly, the in-between
everything about yourself that you hate
every imperfection, every flaw
is something that I stare at you in awe
You fill my every waking moment
and most of my sleeping ones too
You keep me up at night
just like you used to do
The things we share are few and far between
but now all we share are glances from different teams
I need you to listen to me, to hear me our for once
I know I shattered and stomped and tore it all down
but I need you to know that wasn't the real me
That was the me in my dreams
the one who messes up everything
That was the me in my dreams
tripping over my own shoelaces
That was the me in my dreams
the one constantly overthinking
Let me prove to you that I can change
Let me prove to you that I know you
Let me prove to you that you are worth it
That I can be your idea of who I used to be

My Father

My father never told my mother "I love you"
but he did the dishes
when she was falling asleep on the couch.
My father never told my mother "I love you"
but would run her back when she was tired.
My father never told my mother "I love you"
but made sure the house was quiet after work.
My father never told my mother "I love you"
but I could tell he meant it anyways.

My father never told me he loved me
but would let me cuddle up next to him.
My father never told me he loved me
but watched a movie with me every night for 3 years.
My father never told me he loved me
but bought me my favorite shoes.
My father never told me he loved me
but made sure I always knew.

My father was a man of few words
but on those long drives home
we would talk about anything under the stars.
My father was a man of few words
but when spirits loosened his tongue,
he would whisper to me
how pretty my mom looked in the moonlight.
My father was a man of few words
but when I had to say goodbye,
he told me he loved me.

Madi Perry (they/them)
Hot Springs National Park Ranger

Madi Perry is a non-binary queer National Park Service interpretative Park Ranger currently working in traditionally Quapaw, Caddo, and Osage nation lands. They are passionate about nourishing relationships between people and the environment. Their views do not represent the federal government and their poems were written outside of work hours.

Where My Heart Goes When Someone Tells Me To Get Off My Phone

As a young person
of this generation
you often hear folks complain
about how easy we have it
how we don't like to work
and we want everything to be handed to us,
even though we've worked our asses off
to maintain a semblance of hope
in a flailing world,
to remember the flap of a butterfly
and ignore the sting of the bee,
to relentlessly forgive
the "work" previous generations did of

colonizing

destroying

dividing

burning

the world that was once so bright.

I wonder what those older folks think,
if they think at all,
watching the breaking news
in delight or fright
of all that we do
to keep the world turning
and create one brand new.

What Do the Moss Remember?

when i see a hillside of moss
stretching tall towards the light
i wonder
what they are reaching out to tell us.

i'm curious,
what they will remember from this time,
in the world growing so fast away
from the light.

perhaps they recall
what it felt like
to take those first steps
towards their hunger
for life
out of the darkness.

and i wonder what
our queer ancestors,
indigenous & black & trans & & & &
heard when they looked upon the moss
after a cleansing rain.

i wonder how they climbed
towards the sun,
so graciously,
knowing we would still live with them.
knowing that their roots would grow
into the seeds of the room
this room witnessed by strangers walking past
in humid, tick country,

where our youth stand somewhat shy
sharing poems of
family & love & witnessing & & &

if somewhere
those ancestors, resting & being,
glow green,
and marvelous,
like the moss i see upon the hillside,
inviting me to join forward.

I Wish I Were a Tree

I wish I were a tree
curving bark
leaves lit with the glow of warm light.
I'd be so much easier to love if I were a tree,
rooted and grounded,
offering comfort to all,
giver of life,
never needing to receive,
relationships tangled with mycelial mystery.
I am growing tired of myself,
roots sporadically shooting off,
killing parts of myself I cannot
forgive.
I wish I were a tree
so I could hug myself,
love myself,
never stand alone,
but deeply within our ecosystem,
firmly in my place,
never questioning my fate.
I wish
for long twirling limbs
always dancing in the wind,
I could love myself
if I were sticky with sap,
losing leaves in fall,
always knowing that Spring will call.

Christi Starr Sanchez, ROOT (she/they)

Christi Starr is a Cuban, queer creative from South Florida. They received a Bachelors of Arts in linguistics with a Spanish concentration from Florida Atlantic University and a Masters of Sciences in Communication Sciences and Disorders from University of Arkansas Medical Sciences. Christi is a speech language pathologist who loves working with children and changing lives. Christi's passion for poetry was reignited upon walking into Kollective Coffee+Tea a few years ago. While it burns low some days, that romantic and passionate ember is always there.

Natural

When mother told daughter	Daughter told mother when
Beauty was pain	Pain was beauty
Watery eyes	Eyes watery
Pulling hair	Hair pulling
Breaking elastics	Elastics breaking
She meant it	It meant she
Hurt to have	Had to hurt
That hair	Hair that
Natural is	Is natural
Kinky, messy, frizzy	Frizzy, messy, kinky
Difficult, unmanageable	Unmanageable, difficult
Hated, it was	Was it hated
So yes,	Yes, so
Straightened it, dyed it	It straightened, it dyed
Beauty for all	All for beauty
White appearing	Appearing white

Moth Aflame

Covered by the dark, I play
Lost in evening hours
I visit the same flowers
Float about it
Hover in the park, and gaze
Crossed by starry showers
I search to find your tower
Hope about it
When two atoms align along a line of plain sight
When restless photons race at the speed of their own light
A planet's magnetic field can guide a moth in the night
Lured by flame, to see
How it sustains heat
Can I withstand its heat
Or go without it
Drawn by my name, I stay
Caught by burning wings
I sense what fire brings
Glow about it

If a flame is a moth then the moth is the flame
when a flame and a moth die out the same.
If flames call moths then who is to blame?
If flames call moths then who is to blame?
When we catch flame then who is a flame

Shell Shedding

molting cicada
exoskeleton hanging
by its chamomile

Stop For Clematis

traffic stopping bloom
please be patient and make room
I would wait for you

Wish Flowers

suspend disbelief
in hexagonal patterns
your wish may come true

A Tulip's Ring

springless wedding bells
chime faintly deep underground
but I still listen

Sunflower Season

a rough hairy stem
with coarsely toothed leaves defends
thousands of small blooms

The Minds that Wander

for Wednesday Night Poetry

This is a sacred space
where poets race
for a spot on that list
for this mic in their fists

We fill the air with words—
this is our hallowed ground
where I followed the sound
to find the fallen tree
to hear the you in me

We snap and sense we're heard
like Mona's waking dreams
flowing through her conscious streams
We take the path of will
bringing empty cups to fill
We are the minds that wander
It's a journey where neutron stars collide
Our own interplanetary guide

Spades puts on spectacular displays
of energy and matter in the Milky Way
We project present and future
Suzanne bends light and time
to show a circle's just a line

You change as soon as you enter
like plain figures bound to center
We are it's perfect curve
It's worthy of study and great patience
Like Emeryn's math equation
To find the value left unknown
To find the y's in answers shown

We are the proof of work

A lovely enigma even after read two
Betty is a living, breathing haiku
a speaker and teacher of Japanese
a patron, a poet and keeper of bees
We have 4 minutes on the timer
You'll find Lucky's lucky charms
where friends meet with open arms
In laughter or tears, we'll listen to you speak
In 36 years, we've never missed a week
We are a creative stir

Learn from Brian's devastation
the red ink running from his creation
A labor of love leaving our hands
learning to wipe mandalas from sand
We transform when we suffer

We are shaman Ricki's drum
The clicks that come from thumbs
vessels god or chance chose
to bare trauma, bliss, and woe
We're more than nouns, we're verbs
We all put the awe in awesome
Kai's garden full of blossoms
Growth is our only mission
No matter the conditions
We aren't the storms we weather
We are the hearts between
Kollective, The Poet's Loft, Maxine's
We are the spirits destination
not a setting or location
We raise their names with her
We stand upon great shoulders
of those wiser and older
for those who lend their ears
for those no longer here
We are the wings of birds

The Mirror

To see you is to see me
A reflection of my energy
Our view rebounds
In focused eyes

To know you is to look through
A refraction of my own light
The view astounds
And breathes a sigh

Makenzie Hartman (she/her)

Makenzie Hartman is a sophomore at Hot Springs Junior Academy.

Pencil

Thank you, you help with
those long, dreary classes,
those endless thoughts
jotted. You help

show my art and work.
If i lose you, I'm lost.
I don't know what to do.

Not just any pencil,
light yellow, bright pastel pink
eraser. Smooth lead
that leads me ahead.

Ode to you, my pencil.

Life

Life is ever changing
but always there.

The rocks, much like life,
stay. They stay through
everything, through the
reformation of water.

Changed but still there.

They stay through the many trails
of life, and are beautiful.
It might take
a moment to find or
notice, but the rocks
are here, and they are
beautiful
from just being.

samm binns, ROOT (they/them)

samm binns is a poet from Hot Springs, Arkansas. They studied creative writing at the University of Arkansas in Fayetteville, receiving the Sturgis Fellowship that included study abroad in Nepal. A former Writer-in-Residence at the Buffalo National River (2020), they founded the Hot Springs Poetry Festival and now work at the Hot Springs Convention Center. Their current obsessions include Kenji Miyazawa and Tibetan Buddhism.

The earth of my breath dug a black hole.
The mountain sighs like a dog
when my lungs cough up roots and bone.

The fire of my feet scorch the trail's shoulder.
The sunset licks its wounds.

The wind o' my hands embrace a tree.
Clouds whisper and the air tastes like rust.

The water o' my eyes flooded with creek water.
Tears carve ravines in my cheeks.

I wear the space of my ears like bat wings.

More than Human

The marble-eyed goats of Hades
chase me and beg for Chex like kids.

An emu's neck coils like a spring,
dreaming of eating someone's hair.

A turtle poses with a red flower
on its shell. Nature forced to wear
A corporate logo.

Donkeys stand defeated,
Ears sagging like Don Quixote's
Broken windmill blades.
They have fought giants and lost.

Alligators sink into mud
Like statues with a vow of silence.

The wolves have forgotten how to howl.
Lemurs compete in screams,
shouting over a man's announcements.

The raccoon moves like a lazy acrobat.

I am an animal, my bladder full.
And nowhere to pee.

Neelix Barby, ROOT (they/them)

Neelix Barby is a 22-year-old autistic poet, mother, and student. Their poems center around themes of trauma, queerness, nature, and growth. They are working towards a career in conservation fueled by their longstanding love for nature and those that inhabit it. Neelix loves all things nerdy hinted at by their name. They want to make a lasting positive impact on those around them. You can find them on under their name on Facebook or instagram @talaxiann.

Consumes

I am cold
I am tired
I have no desire to speak

Each attempt ends in tension
Deep regret takes hold after each misstep
The rules to this game are an ever-changing roulette
whenever I am certain of my mastery
the wheel spins again

I am tired
The air that hangs between us is cold
I wish I could take apart my skull and peer at the mechanical
source of my systematic failure
A mechanical problem has a concrete solution

I know none will reach for me
When I vanished for half a year
not one word came from that former home
I will fade into a sore subject
An unmarked grave with lichen in place of flowers
at last I am welcomed

The birds sing as the fungi consumes my body
finally turning me into something beautiful

Good Sweat

Clouds of pending rain
overcast the lush green mountain.

Moisture blossoms from my pores.
It is a familiar sensation on my skin.
We have become unwilling companions.

A place lacking in such rich green
draws out the liquid to coat my forehead.
Equations summed in poorly chosen words
drench my back.
A claustrophobic river runs through my brow
with no time to dry as tasks tumble on.

These spigots are different.
This humid brook trickling trails down my cheek. Calm.

Tan Halo

I want to be one of you
I want to exist as you do
Helper, teacher, steward
I yearn for the tan halo
The golden symbol of Earth's protectors
To me that is paradise
I yearn to call it home

Liberty Everhart (she/her)

Liberty Everhart is a Sophomore at the Arkansas School for Mathematics, Sciences, and the Arts. She loves to write poetry and has filled up many notebooks of poems since Sharing Tree Space.

Fireflies

When I was young,
I lived in the countryside.
Acres upon acres of fields,
of trees, of woods, of life
constantly surrounded me.

The summer season was always my favorite.

I would run out in front of the house
by the wood log fence,
by the big sprawling tree
and I would sit in the same spot
that I had worn down with time.

I would watch the sunset
with its peach, golden yellow,
and orange hues and I would wait.

I would wait for the fireflies
that would arise from their soft grassy bed.

After night had fallen, and the moon was high,
and the stars were prominent, I would stand.
And I would begin chasing
the flying, flickering
balls of light.

Window

When you look through this window,
tell me what you see.
In truth, I know you see nothing
for I know that you are blind.

Now tell me what you wish to see;
what wonders so divine?

Days will pass, and days to weeks,
you'll never see outside,
so I'll tell you what lies beyond,
a magic world below.

Over and over again, I'll describe it to you,
the beauties of this world.
While you rest your weary head,
I'll make your imagination swirl.

The Sound of Wet Music

The river is alive
with its own flowing sound
its own special music.

Try all you might to recreate its song,
you'll never get it quite right.
It's part of a natural soundtrack
a favorited element,
a beloved instrument.

The sound of the river,
unique in its own.

The sound of the river,
teeming, with life.

Come,
enjoy this fountain of youth.

Feel alive,
in this sound
of wet music.

Validation

I came from a home
where I am denied.
Last time I came out,
they laughed,
and I cried.

I can't be referred to
as myself
when I'm at school,
because the paperwork
says otherwise.
My friends often forget,
because they met someone else
who wasn't me.

So when I came
to this beautiful cohort,
the meaning in the validation
is immeasurable.

To be called my my name.
To be known as "he" and "they."
It's invaluable.
It's three hours
of comfort
and sanctuary.
It's being true,
and being acknowledged
as human.

Before I return
to my broken home
and have to be known
as "Liberty"
yet have no liberty

or liberations,
and known as "she" and "her."
Before I get dead-named.
Before I get misgendered.
I get this.

To have these three hours,
it keeps me at bat.
To see these gorgeous
human beings
(unless self-identified
as otherwise),
reminds me that change will come.
To see everyone so comfortable
in who they are,
so unapologetically themselves.
To see them introduce themselves
so seamlessly
as the versions of themselves
that they created,
that they discovered
reminds me—
I am human.
I am valid.
I do matter.
And nothing will ever change that.

So here I am, and here I stay.

Mandy Skaggs, ROOT (she/her)

Mandy Skaggs is an academic nerd, perpetual student, treehugger, dog-lover, singer/songwriter, avid reader, would-be world-traveler, National Geographic peruser, spirituality enthusiast, advocate for people with disabilities, and her family's favorite comedian. She grew up alongside two autistic and intellectually disabled older siblings, which impacted her greatly. She graduated from Hot Springs High School in 2014 and received a double bachelors degree in psychology and anthropology in the Spring of 2018 from the University of Central Arkansas. She writes most about the hardships of life that both connect and separate us, but which we do not often speak about in what is considered polite conversation–things we are thinking and feeling without verbalizing very much. Writing is her therapy.

Medusa Down

I was not present the day she fell,
But Medusa is down.

Her branches still slither hither and thither
About her head, stretching,
Reaching for the sky in vain.

Those snakes have found their way to the ground
And smell the soil we have sauntered around.

They hear the melodies of the yellow-bellied,
The cheerful chuckles of children,
And the scratching pens of poets.

Medusa is at rest,
As are her lengthy locks,
As are the birds she has helped to feed.

If Medusa can rest,
Perhaps so can we.

Soft Spring Grasses

After walking on eggshells and down gravel roads,
all of which tore at the best and the worst of shoes,
bruising my toes and slicing the flesh of my heels.
He makes me feel as if I am prancing
on Soft Spring Grasses,
barefoot and wild and brilliant.

I savor the texture against the bottoms of my feet,
a silky smooth cushion to revive my aching soles,
one that encourages me to sprint about freely,
and to appreciate the journeys I take
rather than obsess over the destinations I seek.

Sometimes the goal is not as important
as the steps along the way.
And when he stepped into my way,
I could not help but welcome the obstacles ahead of me,
smile down at the floor upon which we both stood,
and follow in his footsteps toward the sweet,
 comforting grounds.

As the bottoms of our feet meet the meadows,
and collect fragments of the earth,
the softness of the grass soothes me inside and out,
cleansing my energy and healing my spirit,
while reminding me what it means to live.

Thunderclaps

The lightning dances in his eyes.
Two and a half seconds later, the next clap of thunder shakes
the house.
The strike was approximately half a mile away,
But that shake felt so much closer
With him sitting down cross-legged on the carpet
Rocking back and forth in front of the open door.
For if the world has the power
To move the floor,
To bend the trees,
And to roar more wildly than any beast,
And to place white veins into a bloodless sky.
Maybe we *should* drop what we are doing,
Witness what the world has to say.
Shriek and clap the way my brother does,
Perhaps add a dance
In celebration that the earth is still willing to talk to us.

Tree Rings

The Tree Rings Loudly
As I Cross the Forest Floor
To Lead Me Back Home

Emeryn Phillips, ROOT (she/her)

Emeryn Phillips is a born and raised Arkansan poet. A writer from the heart, and collector of the thrifted, she enjoys all that nature has to offer. If any lesson ever stuck, it's that one can always spend more time to reflect on and cherish the peace found in the small wonders of the world.:

More Than A Visage

I am diminished as an ant underfoot,
any power I possess is powerless here,
casting my eyes up the sheer face,
of white water and cragged rock.
The cascade of falling water,
an unrelenting and thunderous roar,
crashing back into itself.
The force of movement,
thrumming like hammer to anvil,
a transfer from potential to kinetic energy.

After marveling skyward long enough,
I find my feet stopped before a still pool,
in awe of the rippling reflection before me.
A still moment following a violent fall.
To see myself,
imperfect.

I kneel at that muddy bank in reverence.
Wishing that I could cup my hands,
lower them in to dispel all I have witnessed,
and drink in that holy lesson.

Homework

Math isn't my thing,
but I'd wager,
as not a maths major,
that one plus one equals two,
and me plus you would be really cute,

because

hearing you talk is my favorite subject.
Could you go too far out on a tangent?
Forget it.
There are no mathematical limits to our conversations,
but if you'd like to run some calculations,
measure the distance between us.
Denote that value so that,
we may subtract, divide, reduce the lengths between,
so that I might observe much closer,
the subtle geometries of your face,
and in the rosy glow of this wonderful space,

find the shapes that make your
quaint
qualities
quantifiable,

let's keep solving equations,
and working at our problems,
trying to figure out the whys (y's)
to all our exes (x's)

until we find an answer that lies,
in a sparkle that shines from the corner of your eyes,
until the distance couldn't be measured in centi, but
millimeters.

Let me trace the angles of your lips,
and not to be obtuse but
I find them to be *quite* acute,

our faces parallel and the odds they intersect?

I think they're pretty good...

I guess the answer is a kiss,
one as significant as pen and paper
working out a moon landing.

You take my breath away,
Physics notwithstanding.

Veda Gonzales (she/her)

Veda Gonzales is a sophomore at Hot Springs Junior Academy and has long roots in the local Wednesday Night Poetry open mic community. Her mother, Tiffany Gonzales, is a published poet.

Lucky One

In valleys deep, where shadows play,
a lucky one, begins its day.
With pines so tall and skies so blue,
it feels the park's embrace anew.

Through the trails, it roams a joyful quest
absorbing nature, a lucky one is truly blessed.
Rustling leaves, a whispered tale,
of mountains high and winding vale.

So here it stands, beneath the sun,
a lucky one, its journey spun.
In nature's realm, it finds its worth,
a tiny speck on this grand Earth.

Rowan Lay, ROOT (he/they)

Rowan is an Arkansas native poet who has been writing for seven years. They are a lover of the natural world, metaphor, and using art to try expressing parts of himself that are still being cultivated. Rowan is hopeful that in sharing poetry, they can share more than just art. He hopes to share a way of looking at the world and at the self with gratitude, healing, authenticity, and growth.

long blades and sweeping stems

ripple
        sway
                cascade

stalks bend
and in the wind
misted salt seafoam
reaches your lips

and the breeze
brings green tide to skin

rings of age in trunk
and i wonder if my heart
grows rings in my soul

i think
i always wanted to grow tall
slender reaching skywards
even higher
than canopy could shade me

in time
however
i have gnarled
knots and twists
and trauma and bliss

and maybe i'll never get any taller
stout and wide and thick
but the fruit in my boughs
has never been sweeter

i think it's clear we'll be
bugs

sorry i meant
birds

sorry i meant
moss

sorry i meant
flowers

sorry i meant
buds

friends

for this natural love
embracing the sensation of
finding peace in the midst of

poetry and art

and breathing free
in this sacred nature

lets soak in our escape from
a world that tells us
we are anything but
beautiful

Kai Coggin, Hot Springs Poet Laureate
(she/her)

Kai Coggin (she/her) is the Inaugural Poet Laureate of Hot Springs, AR, author of five collections, and a recipient of a 2024 Academy of American Poets Laureate Fellowship. She has won numerous awards and fellowships, and her poems have been published in *POETRY, Academy of American Poets, Best of the Net, Prairie Schooner,* and elsewhere. Coggin is a Certified Master Naturalist, a K-12 Teaching Artist in poetry with the Arkansas Arts Council, and host of the longest running consecutive weekly open mic series in the country—Wednesday Night Poetry. www.kaicoggin.com

Water Body

If water never disappears—

if the water on earth
is almost always constant,
cycling infinitely
through ice, rain, tide,
stream, river, vapor, steam
everything in between,

if water never disappears—

we are drinking rainwater
that fell over pyramids,

we are swimming in dinosaur tears
and making tea from ancient seas,

the water in my reusable bottle
could've dripped off the leaves of the oldest tree,

and there is a permanence
in that kind of finite flow,
there is a grounding
in what these precious molecules remember
and what they know.

Human bodies are 60% water,
just think of how far back
your water body goes.

Fleeting

1.

The wind rustles music
through the golden leaves
autumnal on branches,
the crunch underfoot echoes
the song my heart sings,
moss quietly greens on hillsides,
these young people seeing
the world through new eyes,
the music of the breeze
lifting their ears
to a world that has been
around them all along.

2.

After autumn rain,
the ground is littered
with the clothes of summer,
rust, ochres, yellows
strewn underfoot
in the patchwork
of letting go.

Sharing Tree Space

These beautiful open hearts,
bright tender beings
being themselves here
under this shady canopy of trees
filled with birdsong,

their voices echo the wild
with such deep conversation and vulnerability.

I'm leaning up against a thick-bellied pine,
watching poems move through the air
onto their open pages.
They are writing,
and feeling through,
crying and learning,
safe here with me
among these old stones,
these mushrooms and leaves.

I hope this peace never leaves them,
and they always remember

Sharing Tree Space

with me.

Wonder Stick

Walking stick
passed from hand to hand,
from heart to heart
as we walk together
first as strangers in a forest
now intergenerational friends
sharing in wonder—

wonder   bending down to touch soft mosses

wonder   stopping to hear the cardinal song

wonder   pointing up with the walking stick
                at an old growth oak
                spilling her red leaves to the forest floor
                in a radius of glowing autumn

Wonder is a practice that can be learned at any age.
Amazement, a song we all know the words to.

Wonder
passed from hand to hand,
from heart to heart
step by step through the national park trails,
a gaggle of open minds,
roots, trunks, branches, leaves, a green family

walking in wonder,
passing the walking stick like a torch
lighting the dark world,
lighting our way home.

Go outside. Hug a tree. Touch moss. Breathe.

Remember
*you **ARE** nature.*

www.ingramcontent.com/pod-product-compliance
Lightning Source LLC
Chambersburg PA
CBHW042316120626
46547CB00022B/2263